LESSIN'S LESSONS

LESSIN'S LESSONS

ROBERT H. LESSIN

rlessin@gmail.com

Answer to number 100 —

to my three wonderful children,

life has no meaning without them

CONTENTS

INTRODUCTION

" "What have you learned in your life?"

That's a question addressed most often in well timed sound bites, some offered while sober and most while not. It's proffered at milestone events but only, unless you want to irritate everyone, within the confines of a multi- minute speech. It's attempted at one's deathbed but rarely with the energy or clarity to do justice to the challenge. It's distilled on a gravestone in a single line.

I was asked this question at a perfect time in a perfect location – the evening overlooking the Mediterranean – when I had nothing else to do. And I am at an age which feels to be a near perfect reconciliation of experience and recollection. This essay took two days to write and fifty years to live.

I have lived a life noteworthy for its successes and its failures. I've had the ability to assess both with neither shame nor envy.

I've long resided at the pinnacle of Wall Street, but sometimes found my residency to be tenuous. I've been one of our country's most prolific venture investors with some achievements and many disappointments. I've been extremely ill and recovered more than people know. I've seen much of the world. And through each experience I've netted not much more than a collection of insights.

I define legacy to be no more and no less than one's teachings; I have three wonderful children and were I to leave only this behind I would be fine. If they can avoid just one of my mistakes from reading this essay, then it will have been worth the effort. And if others wish to eavesdrop, so be it.

ONE

MY YOUTH

1. **Economic under privilege combined with intellectual over privilege is a "killer" combination.** The scene is a near perfect depiction of my childhood. My twin brother, Steve, and I, only 12 years old, perspire as we carry our skis up Wildcat Mountain, one of the more formidable ski areas in the East. And to make sure we don't miss the indignity of it all, we do so directly under the lift line. We need only look up to be reminded how differently others enjoy this pasttime. And, when we lack the energy to look up, we need not wait long for the melted snow of the skiers above to pelt our jackets.

My father is having us walk not to improve our conditioning, nor teach us humility, but to save the cost of a lift ticket. Despite our love of this activity, it won't be for many years until we are bought a (half-day) ski pass. My Mom will never be bought a ski ticket; she will wear my Father's parka when he goes in for lunch.

We will always live in the worst neighborhood of the best town. We are thus continually reminded of our social standing while, admittedly, imbued with terrific educations.

I have a forever burning desire to leave the economic circumstances of my childhood.

2. Self dignity is the only source of lasting happiness. Steve was blessed with skills of which I could only dream. No athletic accomplishment withstood his focus. He embraced outlying culture long before it became mainstream. His intellectual pursuits were keen, if not unusual.

But his curse was that Steve's interests did not align with those of my Father while mine overlapped seamlessly. I was praised incessantly while my brother was degraded. Other relatives took up the call. My Mother was too weak to rebuke this assault.

Ironically, skiing became my brother's passion. One day, inexplicably, I ski better than he. For many decades, he never skis again.

3. Follow your passion, no matter how much of an outlier. At Harvard College, I have a difficult time getting a date. The school tries to avoid hierarchy, but my public education underscores my uninspired lineage. My intelligence is at the right end of a continuous curve but not discontinuous like many of my classmates who think fundamentally differently.

Long before I know the concept of target marketing I decide to learn to ballroom dance. It is the late 70's; I will stand out. Each Tuesday and Thursday evening I take the subway and dance with those two generations my senior. I learn to dance very well and differentiate myself with those few classmates who care.

A year later, I'm attending Harvard Business School and interviewing for jobs on Wall Street. I'm asked by all firms why I want to be an investment banker. I have no idea. I've never known one. The interviewers don't look to be the type who would find my "Wildcat" story to be endearing. No matter how mediocre the investment bank, none of which longer exist, I make it into no second interviews.

But Morgan Stanley, which is then the cream of the industry, is intrigued by my fondness for ballroom dancing. To their credit, they have come to the conclusion that, in order to thrive, they must find outliers. I am offered Morgan's only summer internship at Harvard. It is one of a handful of events that fundamentally defines my life. For the second (and one of my last) time ever I will be wearing a suit.

Often, I ski Tuesday through Friday in my second year of business school. My career, at least near term, has been clarified. Having just graduated Harvard College I know how to pass exams. I don't like lift lines.

I will graduate HBS with no honors and no distinctions. But I will graduate.

TWO

MORGAN STANLEY

4. Jump out of the starting gate; there will always be time to rest later. Soon, way sooner than anyone suspects, I will start my career at Morgan Stanley. I have the most prestigious job on campus. Relaxed and rested, I am raring to begin.

I commit to my permanent career at the end of my summer. My commitment is unambiguous and on the spot. I play no games, a mentality that will be discussed later.

I chose to begin my career before I graduate. Morgan is confused but desperate for support. While others are summering in Europe I will be developing a reputation. It is impossible not to be perceived as the best when you're the only one present. I will have worked with many by the time my colleagues arrive. And the Firm, out of guilt, will pay for me to attend my graduation.

5. If you don't "jump out of the gate", take your time. Our caretaker in Colorado took the exact opposite approach. He made no early career decisions choosing instead to wander. He appears every bit as happy as I. He merely reversed the order of our lives. The key, on reflection, is not starting early or late; just avoid congestion.

6. Get yourself a mentor. I am assigned to a transaction, Marsh & McLennan buying C.T. Bowring, which is, and may always be, the most complex transaction ever undertaken. It is a hostile, transatlantic exchange offer requiring both US and UK regulatory approval.

It will take two years of my life. I will develop cancer (Hodgkin's) in the interim, leave each evening to be radiated and return each night to work while London awakes. I am distracted from my ailment by the demands of the project. Jack Regan, the CEO of the client, is confused by the audacity of a young associate leaving his evening strategy meetings; he learns of my ailment by barging unannounced into my hospital room the morning after my operation to remove my malignant lymphnode.

The Morgan team dwindles as the deal goes on. Ultimately, the deal will last for two years and the Morgan team will become just Bob Greenhill and me. The other advisors, including Joe Flom and Gershon Kekst who, along with Bob Greenhill, are three of the five luminaries who created the modern day merger business (the other two being Marty Lipton and Felix Rohatyn), become lasting friends. Bob becomes something between my father figure and my father.

The phone rings late in the fall of 1979 - our deal has been approved by Lloyds. The last condition has been met; we can close the transaction. I am elated but I soon realize that a different phone call would have meant that I wasted two years. I would have had nothing to show for 10 percent of my life.

Naida does not believe that I am deferring our marriage only because I was waiting for the deal to clarify. She is the only Wellesley student who purchases a subscription to the Wall Street Journal; she intends to confirm my representation. The day of the announcement she runs down the corridors of her dormitory, clutching the newspaper and screaming, "I'm getting married!"; her fellow students think that she's lost it.

I then vow never to be beholden to one event again. I go the other extreme, working on hundreds of transactions at one time. It makes me a flawed executioner of assignments but it also enables me to see trends that others can't. Most importantly, my sense of self respect is never again prisoner to a single event.

Years later, I ask Michael Price, my friend and star banker at Evercore, to what he attributes his professional success. Michael had not one, but four luminary mentors – Michael David-Weill, Felix Rohatyn, Steve Rattner and Roger Altman. His response was as inelegant as it was honest – "I knew how to suck my mentors dry."

7. Get global exposure. Before Morgan, I had been to Europe once. As a college graduation present, my buddy and I had bought bicycles with the intent of spending our summer cycling around Europe. After two days of cycling the terrain steepened; we purchased Eurail passes and portaged our bikes. We wouldn't ride again until the terrain flattened in Denmark.

I was asked by my parents to call them once, around mid-summer, to check in. I was told that they would reject my collect call if they had nothing significant to report. I had much to tell them when I called in late July. For days I practiced condensing my insights into a three minute conversation.

I telephoned from the Viennese Post and my collect call was rejected. In later years, with the need to rectify this episode's psychological damage, I realized that it was the most expensive call I would ever make.

During the Marsh Mac transaction, I had the occasion to go to London often – sometimes two times a week. It was an effort by the other side to wear us down. We would be summoned to London with the stated intention of negotiating a deal. Then they would change their mind.

They didn't know Bob Greenhill who was never fazed by this illusion. And they didn't appreciate how then easy it was to get between New York and London with the Concorde. But we never saw Europe and we rarely saw the outside of Warburg's conference rooms. I did, however put on a lot of weight having never before been exposed to either Port or Stilton.

A year later, I'm sitting in a conference room as a senior associate and Dick Fisher, the to-be-CEO of the Firm, and Bob Greenhill, the to-be-President, ask that I relocate to Europe. Morgan has about thirty people in Europe (which grew to be about ten thousand) and they want to fortify their operations. They also want to assess why it is that their European business is so weak. This will turn out to be another event that defines my life.

The latter question is easy. Morgan Europe is then run by a patrician who is not unknown to start his day when he's served his lunch and end his day when he's finished reading the *Financial Times*. What to do about it is more complicated. I bring over an analyst, who himself later becomes quite noteworthy in the financial community, and we decide that we will present US acquisition ideas to European companies. It is, in retrospect, a ridiculous idea – in 1981 Europe is in recession and the dollar is strong – a perfect combination to assure no interest. But, even though the Morgan Stanley name is not then well known in Europe, and I am 26, we are seen by the top levels of nearly every company in Europe, probably for entertainment value.

We work hard. We arrive early and are still calling New York in the hours after they, with a five hour time difference, have left. We are largely ignored by bankers other than Bob Greenhill who visits us every two months. In two years we bring in one piece of business.

But, for an American, I become incredibly comfortable with non-US cultures.

8. Don't confuse professional and personal happiness. After two years, I'm called back to the US. I am done so on a Friday afternoon with the expectation that I will report to work on Monday morning. Months ago in London my first child was born. We had just purchased our first home (bought for $300k and sold later, by someone else, for £40mm) with the signed contract to move in on Tuesday.

Dutifully, I showed up in New York for work on Monday. Morgan had remembered to arrange everything except to tell me what to do. Most importantly, they gave me no clients. With nothing to do, I called a recently formed entity called KKR, then its arch rival – Forstmann Little, then all the wannabes.

I changed the mandate of my newly formed group from coverage to idea generation. Financial buyers, unlike European corporations, live for proprietary ideas. For a long time we were the source of nearly all the Street's acquisition ideas. My group became the training ground of many future leaders of the financial community.

I went from the least to, far and away, the most profitable banker at Morgan Stanley. When asked why I wasn't ecstatic, I noted that, had I vested my ego in my business success a year ago, I would have killed myself.

9. Front end your work day. My day starts at my desk (not to be confused with at home) at 4am. There is a fascinating New York City subculture at that hour. I figure, rightly, that you can't help but look intelligent with a 5 hour head start. It also enables me to put my children to bed (and, as my divorce later confirms, leaves energy for little else). I keep this schedule for 15 years.

It is compromised slightly when co-workers arrive at 5 or 6am to assure that they get to see me; I have no interest in seeing them – I want to think. But what are you going to do – ask them to wait 4 hours?

The less exotic reason I begin my day so early is that, living in New Jersey, I intend to avoid the morning rush hour. A quarter of a century later I still avoid the morning rush hour, although at the back end rather than the front end.

10. At some point, you can't go back. I was psychologically equipped to deal with social outliers; that made me incapable of dealing with executives of utilities, insurance companies, banks and established energy companies. It's now quite embarrassing that I understand nothing of these industries; but it's too late. I was too good at sidestepping what didn't interest me and I will always be a lesser banker for having done so.

11. Be a Vice Chairman. At the age of 31, I become Morgan Stanley's youngest partner ever. I run private equity, media and retail – a collection of industries whose only commonality is that they have companies that are run by "characters". I oversee the bank's deal flow. Bob Greenhill wants me to run the investment bank at the age of 35 but others believe me to be too young. I am given the title of Vice Chairman of the Investment Bank, a title with no direct responsibility and one to which I will aspire the rest of my career.

Over time, I develop a clear sense of organizational hierarchy consistent, not with ego, but with what resonates with me. "Vice Chairman" is my most desirable title followed by "Chairman" then "CEO". "President" is, for me, the least desirable job in an organization. You have to know what's really going on. Fortunately, no one who knows me, would ever subject their organization to that.

12. Don't confuse professional and personal loyalty. In early 1993, on zero notice, the entire Firm is required to be on a phone call where Bob Greenhill, after 31 years, announces his retirement. I'm amazed. How could it be that he never hinted at this? I was just skiing with him yesterday. It turns out he was the victim of a high stakes political battle. The Firm-wide memo distributed later that day is well known within Morgan Stanley for its indifference and lack of graciousness—it will always be known as "31 words for 31 years".

The background of this evolution will go to my grave. Suffice it to say, don't confuse professional and personal loyalties.

For quite a while the new management of Morgan Stanley presumes that is the end of Bob Greenhill's career, and for a while it is.

13. Foster relationships when others need you, not when you need them. What the new management never understood about Bob Greenhill was his fierce loyalty, often to a fault. And his loyalty was never more obvious than when others walked away. Such was the case with Sandy Weill.

Sandy, as head of Shearson Lehman, had been treated internally, I'm told, as unceremoniously as Bob had been at Morgan Stanley. He was abandoned by most everyone but Jamie Dimon and Bob. I recall stories of Sandy, without a job, flying Peoples Express, Bob on the aisle and Sandy in the middle seat, looking for Sandy's next employer.

And when Bob left Morgan, it was Sandy who came to his rescue. Sandy then ran Primerica whose only known brand (to anyone with more than a five digit income) was Smith Barney. Smith Barney was a once glorious bank that had long been marginalized. It was quite a coup for Smith Barney when Bob accepted Sandy's offer to run it (it turned out as much a coup for Bob as it was for Sandy who, prior to Jamie, became known as the world's leading financier).

But Bob had long learned his limitations and he needed staff. We had dinner in the spring of 1993 where Bob asked me to leave Morgan Stanley and join him as Vice Chairman to run the investment bank for Smith Barney.

I had a terrific future at Morgan Stanley. I had enormous admiration for Dick Fisher, Morgan's recently appointed CEO. But I decided that personal loyalty, to Bob, trumped institutional loyalty, to Morgan Stanley, and I left.

15. No one is bigger than their institution. In the summer of 1995, we were awarded the Koor IPO mandate. Koor was not a company; it was, effectively, a country. Specifically, it represented 10 percent of the Israeli economy. It was a coup that Smith Barney had been chosen to lead their IPO. It was an honor for me that I would be spearheading their deal.

We exposed the company to our accounts. The transaction, largely because of the appeal of Benny Gaon, the CEO, was proceeding fine. On November 4th, in the middle of the roadshow, Yitzhak Rabin was assassinated. Few individuals had so represented the dreams of their country.

We huddled for hours. This wasn't about an IPO. It was about whether Israel had matured to be bigger than one person, even Yitzhak Rabin.

I chose to go forward and the deal was completed successfully. For awhile I became a mini hero in the Israeli business community. But these things don't last – I now can't even get my Chinese Malaysian partner a visa to visit the country.

16. Don't miss paradigm shifts. In a few years, Smith Barney, for me, began to lose its interest. Most every client had been transitioned. Bob had a falling out with Jamie and left. And Mike, who often served as a scapegoat, departed.

I had since decided that, finally, I would not accompany Bob. First, Sandy had drafted Bob's lucrative departing contract such that it was illegal for me and Bob to now work together. Second, recently, I had a dream whereby Bob, who was a very accomplished pilot, had crashed his jet with me aboard. That didn't bother me – what bothered me was the next day's imagined headline that "Bob Greenhill and a colleague were killed yesterday in a plane crash." I no longer wished to be "a colleague".

And Bob Greenhill, for all his loyalty, was not the most nuanced person you'll ever meet.

At Morgan Stanley, he learned of my wife's therapy because he had to approve her monthly trips back to New York. Bob was uncomfortable; I thought here we are moving from New York City; it was not exactly pioneering to have a psychiatrist. But, besides being uncomfortable, Bob reckoned he could deal with the issue himself.

We all skied together frequently in Mirabel. One trip Bob disrupted the ski lift line to get himself close to Naida. Ultimately achieving his objective (no small feat for those who have skied in Europe) he looked her squarely in the eye and ordered: "Think positive!"

They broke the mold when they created Bob; I would miss him.

But what really transitioned my interest was, through Mosaic, the evolution of the Internet. In 1995, my then brother-in-law exposed me to the Internet.

It took no great vision to realize that any system that enabled the dissemination of information anywhere in the world, at any time and at no cost, would fundamentally change the workings of the world.

Interestingly, I had been exposed to the concept of the Internet the year before with my banking of General Magic. Marc Porat, who is the brother of one of my then dearest friends, had created General Magic which, leveraging a bewildering collection of global partners, effectively was the "closed" Internet. Marc and his company were the hottest commodities in Silicon Valley until the real Internet came along and, in brief order, wiped them out.

Upon embracing the Internet, I did two things. I sent a Lotus Notes message around to all our bankers announcing that all my future disseminations would be electronic; if anyone cared to know what was on my mind (which then, unlike now, they did) they best learn Lotus Notes. Without having a name for what I had done, I learned the distinction between "opt in" and "opt out."

I wrote a book entitled *The Middle Chapters*. Its premise was that the early and the later years of the Internet could be envisioned; it was the middle years that would define its relevance. The general themes were as insightful as the specific examples were flawed. But Smith Barney published the book and did not allow it to be disseminated outside its client base.

I really believed what I wrote, in its relevance not only for technology developments but for personal career tracks as well; it would be hypocritical not to move on. The last thing to do was negotiate with Jamie my departure.

FOUR

WIT CAPITAL

Andy Klein is a brilliant lawyer who was meant never to practice. Graduating from Harvard Law School he worked briefly for Cravath, Swaine & Moore. But his real passion was to challenge the conventional, a death sentence for a corporate lawyer.

He formed a microbrewery which had all the necessary ingredients but capital. But rather than raise capital conventionally he chose, working with the SEC, to do so online. So it was that Wit Capital was born.

But it lacked a reputation and I lacked a job. I agreed both to invest $5 million and to head (not to be confused with "to run") the company.

It's amazing how briefly $5 million lasts when you're talking about revolutionizing the capital markets. My first priority was to raise capital and thereby build a Board of Directors. Never has there been such a stellar Board for any company, let alone one that, as of then, had no business.

At our Board meetings, sitting around our coffee table on the sixth floor of The Strand Bookstore, would be Joe Gleberman (representing Goldman Sachs, a 10% shareholder), Steve Gluckstern (representing Capital Z and, himself, the founder of reinsurance), Joe Flom (the dean of the legal profession), John Fisher (one of our nation's best early stage venture investors), Bill Ford (one of our nation's best later stage venture investors), Gil Mauer (president of Hearst), Ed Fleischman (ex-commissioner of the SEC) and Joe Hardiman (former chief of the NASD).

A large number of the financial community climbed the six flights in Union Square which we were renting at $8 per square foot. I particularly remember entertaining Dick Grasso, then head of the NYSE. Ashamed of our surroundings, I had asked my assistant, Michelle, to hang some of my collection of newspaper clippings from noteworthy days. Dick was, after all, head of the NYSE; I wanted to impress him. We all sat in lawn chairs as I began explaining my vision. I never did regain my composure when I saw that every picture that Michelle had hung was a depiction of a famous market crash.

17. Everyone is handed a few breaks. Success is defined by who recognizes, and then capitalizes, on them. But what we really needed was a client. We had been put frequently into syndicates that would pay for a cup of coffee (this before the prevalence of Starbucks). We needed one client to put us "on the cover".

And we found that in Earthweb. All investment banks understood that it would take one break to legitimize us. All knew to walk away if we were offered a co-manager position. And no issuer, rightly so, would trust us alone.

But the dot.com world was getting very hot – and JP Morgan had, up until then, missed the trend. When they threatened to walk if we were on the cover, Jack Hidary, the founder and CEO of Earthweb, said that would be fine. They caved.

We were given no economics but we could care less – we had a precedent. We shamelessly then always asked to be a co-manager (this time with economics) and would point to precedent "like, I don't know, Earthweb."

Within one year we had been a co-manager on dozens of deals and gone public. Within two years, the company was worth $4.5 billion. I remember entering Sea World at one stock price and leaving a few hours later, $50 million (on paper) richer.

18. Take advantage of an appreciated stock to buy real businesses. AOL gets all the credit for using a "new economy" company to buy a "real" company. So too should we. We exchanged the Wit stock for shares in SoundView, a "real" company focused on real technology banking. Our dilution was de minimis but we were one degree too clever – we had pissed off the SoundView shareholders who aligned perfectly with their employees whom we needed to retain. It ended up killing both companies.

19. Don't confuse luck with brilliance. I never took the time to reflect on how tied our fate was to NASDAQ and the overheated IPO market. When NASDAQ cracked so too did we. Upon reflection, I would have owned my shares in Wit and sold ETF's (or its equivalent as ETF's had not yet been created) on NASDAQ. I would have isolated our performance from factors beyond our control. But of course I never did and will never have the chance to do so with such materiality again.

20. Don't believe your own B-S. I couldn't believe the stock's decline. I had come to so believe our story. I bought the stock aggressively until it was ultimately sold for near cash value. Like many CEO's I made the mistake of believing my own B-S.

The ultimate dispassionate investor has to be Jason Porat, Marc's eldest then twelve year old son. Marc, as both an engaged father and a consummate showman, bought both of his children one share of General Magic stock at its IPO. The stock, not surprisingly, opened up strong and Marc called Jason and asked if he wanted to sell his share. "Don't be ridiculous Dad—I have great faith in you." Throughout the day, it continued to strengthen; Marc asked Jason again. "Dad—you and I are forever in this together." Toward the end of the day, with the stock more than 50% higher than the opening, Marc, out of courtesy, asked again. Without hesitation Jason screamed "SELL!" The stock never saw a higher price; Jason was one of the few shareholders who ever made money with General Magic.

And while you are at it, don't believe anyone else's B-S either. Upon joining Smith Barney I was interviewed by a leading business periodical. In short order, it became apparent that the "journalist" was intent on writing a story whose essence was that the Morgan team was both overcompensated AND incompetent. Facts would not be standing in her way. I explained that her facts were wrong and her misrepresentations might damage my young children. She was indifferent to the former and appeared not displeased by the latter. I hope that this journalist has become wildly successful; I'd like her to feel what it's like to sit on the other side of the table.

21. Don't get promoted ahead of your accomplishments. Acknowledging that over promotion has some real leverageable business benefits, I view it, ultimately, as a "net negative". I nearly lost control of Smith Barney's investment bank when my "outsized" salary was disclosed. I did effectively lose Wit when we overplayed our hand in buying SoundView. Over-promotion is fine - until your first misstep; then the pent up resentment pours out and the feedback loops work in reverse.

I'm a believer in President Obama; I travel too much not to know what it means to be globally respected. I spend too much time teaching talented students residing in the inner city not to understand the hope that he engenders. But I'm also in the camp that believes that it would have been better had he deferred his acceptance of the Nobel Peace Prize.

Of course, over-promotion sometimes comes with a different agenda. Naida and I separated toward the end of my tenure running Wit Capital; when that happened, I merely skimmed the articles about me. But the pictures-that's where I focused.

22. Don't assess an investment just by its financial return. By the end of the Wit saga, I had made very little money. Most I had given back by continually buying a free falling stock. I'm asked often would I do it again. Without any attempt at justification the answer is, of course – it gave me the front row seat to the new economy. I will have an answer when my grandchildren ask what I did during the birth of the new economy.

FIVE

VENTURE INVESTING

While acknowledged as one of the leading East Coast venture investors, that is equivalent to labeling me as the "smartest utility executive". It doesn't mean very much. I've made hundreds of venture investments, lost on most and made on a few. I'm not sure that I've generated a net positive return. I'm sure that I've generated tax write-offs. I also have a fabulous wardrobe of T-shirts from now defunct internet start-ups. One of the unanticipated benefits of heading Wit is that I'm Chairman of Dawntreader, a leading East Coast early stage venture fund. It's taken too long to realize returns but, ultimately, my investors will be happy.

What I've learned in venture capital can be summarized as follows:

23. Business, unlike biology, tends toward <u>dis</u>equilibrium. This may summarize my entire knowledge of business. When you're hot in venture capital, everything goes your way. You attract and retain the best employees with the least dilution. You raise the cheapest capital. Reference customers are excited to adopt your technology. And when the circumstances turn, it all goes the other way. There may be a concept of equilibrium but you're long bankrupt. The key is to leverage the positive cycle to be strong enough to withstand the negative.

24. Don't confuse what should be with what will be; adoption takes way longer than you think. Most of my investments went bankrupt because we misestimated the time for adoption. Long before there was Web MD, there was Medtech. Long before there was Vista Print there was iPrint. And long before there was Facebook, there was Six Degrees. I was a meaningful investor in all three. We just never had the capital to see our vision through.

25. Entrepreneurs dilute themselves way too much and way too early. Question – how do you obtain a couple of points of ownership in a venture company? Answer – create the idea, form the company, start with 100% ownership and rapidly get diluted to 4%. In reality, that's what often happens. Either the company raises money too quickly or the idea is too capital intensive. And, just to make sure you are totally pissed off, the investors' shares are different than yours – they get paid back first.

One of the keys to venture capital is judging when to raise money. Too soon and you will dilute yourself unnecessarily, too late and you will go bankrupt.

There are many reasons why Bill Gates is where he is and the rest of us are where we are. Obviously he had a great idea, but there are other "killer apps". The key, in my mind, is that he never raised outside capital until the IPO.

26. Let others do your marketing. In a world of perfect connectivity, it does not make a lot of sense to spend non-targeted marketing dollars. Put the money into the product and let the blogs do the marketing for you. That's what my son has done with his highly successful drop.io. Too bad that General Motors never thought about this; its mindset cost all of us $50 billion.

27. There are no new ideas, just recycled ideas whose time has come. Long before there was Facebook we created Six Degrees (Andrew Weinrich created it. I was a Director and first round investor). The concept behind Six Degrees has similarities to Facebook but Six Degrees failed where Facebook is thriving and, according to my son, may someday dominate the digital world. The reason is not just a refined concept. It has to do with the fact that, when we launched Six Degrees, memory was incredibly expensive and there was no way to monetize traffic (online advertising barely existed). We had 1.5 million members and we quietly pleaded that no more would join. Ultimately, like most great concepts, we ran out of money.

28. Run your business and your life as a variable cost. It was supposed to be my eldest son's first experience with global humiliation. Online viewers gawked as he and his friends, labeled as the young technological glitterati, partied in Northern Cyprus while the world's economy was in free fall. Each blog entry was more hostile than the last as they sought to outdo themselves in criticizing my son's insensitivity.

Never mind that this week of alleged indulgence had been orchestrated months before. Never mind that the cost to the participants, including airfare, was likely less than the cost of their remaining home. It was the online analogy to Bruce Wasserstein gracing the cover of Forbes months before the financial world's collapse in the early 1990's.

But it got me thinking. How does my son now live his life? And, more importantly to others, is there a construct to his lifestyle that is relevant, not just to his generation, but to mine?

Sam took a keen interest in my successes and my even greater failures. He learned the concept of adoption. He was brought to many of my corporate meetings to add the perspective of how a teenager would view their online initiative. In short order the CEO's would seek his guidance and ignore mine. I told myself that was because he was more age appropriate. It was probably because he is smarter. He was surprisingly bi-lingual speaking "traditional" and "new". He was, as Tom Glocer, head of Thomson Reuters would label him, "Lessin 2.0".

And it is this background that explains the underlying thesis of how Sam lives his life – he lives it as a variable cost. What do I mean by this – that his entire personal and professional cost structure is variable; it is dependent on his successes and failures and can be eliminated at any time. His fixed "burn rate" is close to zero.

Living a life of variable cost does not mean living life cheaply. Nor does it mean living life virtually. It means that you have the ability to cheaply and efficiently customize your cost structure to reflect your financial needs, your financial capability and the financial environment at that time. It means that your costs move naturally with your revenues. It means not being compelled to liquidate illiquid assets, partially because you don't have any.

I should have seen this coming when he conceived of Life Capital. The highest fixed expense for a young adult is their education. Sam created LifeCapital.com where individuals could sell a piece of their future income for up front capital. His reasoning was that, if individuals could sell debt in their future (i.e. student loans), why could they not sell equity (that is, allow investors to own a minority interest in individuals with capped return and non-voting stock)?

He would leverage the Internet so that the recipient could put forth his/her investment thesis online and the investors could invest in individuals of like interest – i.e. self-interested mentors.

Long exposed to the problems of adoption, I feared that the adoption cycle here would be measured in decades and not years. But Sam was passionate and forged ahead. What was not a variable expense was web development and the now-defunct web developer generated a little code and a lot of write-offs.

I didn't appreciate it then. I'm not sure that Sam did. But he was adopting his early focus on a life of variable costs.

To live a life of true variable cost, one needs a number of factors intact:

-Perfect information – a variable life requires timely, pervasive and perfect information so that the appropriate decision for that moment can be made. The Internet was critical. Wireless broadband is required because decisions must be actionable at all times. So is location based information as one's location often directly affects one's choices.

-Recession – a recessionary environment puts a premium on last minute decisions. Ultimately, as the moment of such decision approaches, the value of excess service inventory approaches zero. One cannot live a variable cost existence in an economic environment where there is the risk of frequent full capacity.

-Deflation – a deflationary environment further encourages deferral of decisions and, when necessary, short term decisions over long term ones. For now, although not necessarily for that much longer, this is our environment.

-Mentality – you cannot define your own success by the accumulation of your assets.

The cost structure of my life, and most of my generation, is anything but variable. As one ages, fixed costs are apt to replace variable costs until, in later years, the process will likely reverse itself. I'm probably at the point of maximum fixed costs.

In an economy with vast compression of assets, and the reality that these assets most likely are financed with short term cash flow (like a salary), this is a deadly combination. We are in the process of massively deleveraging our society and asset values will compress for many years. Assets will have to be liquidated exactly when they can't. Many of my colleagues will lose large percentages of the wealth that they accumulated over many years. I don't know that Sam saw this coming but he did not define his success by the accumulation of assets and he did foresee the technology that makes a variable life possible.

"Home", for Sam, was a relatively modern multi-story apartment building in lower New York City. A majority of Sam's classmates make Manhattan their first stop after graduation and most have not yet found a reason to leave. While technology enables connectivity, there remains a clear preference to supplement this with ready physical contact. And the few that opted out of New York City find reason to pass through on a regular basis.

Sam, unlike me, did not make the mistake of confusing technology with a virtual existence. Upon grasping that technology enabled isolation, I gravitated immediately to a hermitic life. Part of this was based on my medical realities, like a major stroke, but most of it was not. It turned out, for me, to be an unsatisfactory existence. I now crave human interaction. Work, for me, is largely my excuse to interact with my friends.

Sam's doorman apartment appeared to reflect some degree of early success. Of course he didn't own the apartment; no one of his generation does. But, unlike his colleagues, neither did he lease it. To do so would entail down payments and monthly rental obligations. It would be unwindable with some difficulty and financial pain. It would be inconsistent with the concept of a variable cost existence. When he stayed in New York, which was most days, he slept in the corner of an apartment which had been formally rented by one of his equally successful classmates. Sam's space was once an oversized living room, needed by neither him nor his roommate. A slab of mason board, some nails, and a few hours, and it became Sam's room.

So far, I have described nothing disconnected from many young adults. What was different was Sam's financial arrangement with his roommate. He paid for his lodging on a nightly (variable) basis, not with the formality that one rents an overnight hotel room but with the loose arrangement that two long time friends settle up an obligation at the end of the month.

Within the apartment, he had neither phone line nor television; both involve registration and monthly costs. His only phone, like many young adults, was wireless and his laptop was the source of all his digital entertainment. When such entertainment required the Internet, which it often did, his connectivity was "borrowed" from his roommate.

Recently, Sam's roommate informed Sam that the arrangement was up – he would be moving in with his girlfriend. Sam dealt with this conceptual setback by identifying an almost as variable, and even more imbalanced, market – subletting.

Since evolving from a nomadic life, humans are encumbered by two embedded instincts – gathering and nesting. A sublet is contrary to both these innate desires and is priced as such. You live amongst the belongings of another and, not only do you not own your quarters, there is no formal acknowledgment that you even rent it. It makes for a highly inefficient market with very short commitment – i.e. perfect for Sam. He pledges to the renter for the same month that they pledge to him. For a greatly reduced payment he gladly accepts the risk that he, and his few digital belongings, may be asked to leave on short notice.

As far as residential New York is concerned, Sam has no relationship to our city. He does this, not to avoid taxes, which he pays religiously (another variable cost) but because relationships and fixed costs are interchangeable concepts.

His transportation cost, like most New Yorkers but unlike most of the country, is not only variable but negligible. He headquartered his company in DUMBO, directly over the Brooklyn Bridge. He can readily walk there without unanticipated delays. When not walking, his subway expense is, of course, variable.

Like to all New Yorkers, the city has its appeal only if it can be freely escaped. For a brief while, Sam had a car in the city. But this entailed a large fixed cost (parking in a garage) or even larger variable (parking tickets and retrieving your car at the impound). The cost of transportation as a variable cost (i.e. car rental) was way too inconvenient, "lumpy" (requiring full day commitments) and expensive. But along came Zipcar and a fixed cost became a variable cost.

In concentrated, youthful North American cities, Zipcar affords its members the convenient opportunity to rent a vehicle on an hourly basis. In fairness, Zipcar itself, functions on a business model 100% antithetical to Sam's. Requiring a critical mass of vehicles, it has enormous fixed cost which, like Fresh Direct, it will attempt to amortize through massive utilization. It requires substantial capital, which is in short supply these days, but does throw off significant cash if used actively within a community. It is as likely to be Webvan (the 1990's poster child for "fixed cost" disasters) as it is to be a Fresh Direct.

"Sam's car", which is neither technically nor emotionally his, now resides in the driveway of my ex-wife's house.

Clothing, for Sam's generation, is inversely correlated with stature. Any profession that correlates formal attire with success (like investment banking) is of zero interest to him (and me). His cost of maintaining his clothing (i.e. cleaning) is not variable but it is de minims. Putting environmental issues aside, the cost of cleaning his clothing, in fact, is competitive with replacing it.

It would be unfortunate to reside in downtown New York and not participate in its culinary delights. But eating is, for all of us, the ultimate variable cost. Satisfying caloric intakes, with the prevalence of fast food, can be achieved at very low cost. Enjoying dining beyond that is a variable cost decision.

So Sam's fixed cost of residing in New York, arguably the most expensive city in America, comes down to his monthly cell phone/blackberry bill – or $80 per month. All of his months have a "burn rate" well beyond that, but they need not. And if he determines that New York is not the right place to be at that stage in his life, the cost of unwinding his life in New York is pretty close to zero. It's a long way from the images of his party.

His creation of drop.io was, in retrospect, way less disconnected from his past than one might otherwise think. Networking had long been a part of his life. He watched Six Degrees thrive and then implode. From college, he is friends with many early employees of Facebook. But, most directly relevant, he had created Kinjunction as a means for our family to electronically and privately share its insights and experiences. I embraced Kinjunction immediately and wrote prolifically each day. The problem was that no other family member had the time to write or even read it. It became for me a glorified diary.

But to Sam it was the linchpin to drop.io. What society was missing, in his view, were private locations (drop spots) where small groups could share digital insights without fear of being snooped on by others. I hadn't appreciated then how important it is for my son's generation to share privately in a world where information, most all of which is searchable, is retained cheaply and forever (I'm told that, in Mexico, students are opting out of Facebook because they fear that it gives too much information to potential kidnappers). "Drop" was chosen because of the analogy to a physical drop spot. "Io" was an analogy for either input/output or the Indian Ocean (i.e. finding the information is as difficult as finding a drop in the Indian Ocean. "Io" is, in actuality, the suffix assigned to the Indian Ocean). I would have nothing to do with it for many reasons including that no one could ever claim (legitimately) that Sam was a direct beneficiary of my relationships.

The success of Google had taught Sam two things. First, the user experience has to be clean and simple. Second, technology, not marketing, now defines the success of an online launch. But even without marketing expenses, some capital would be required. He turned naturally to his friends at RRE. Sam had a fantastic experience working one summer at RRE. Draper Fisher Gotham, the other leading NYC early stage venture firm, soon followed. Drop.io is now taking off. Its global acceptance, both with individuals and enterprises who wish to conduct private exchanges of text, pictures and video, is growing dramatically.

But this is not an observation about drop.io no matter how proud I am (there are enough blogs and articles that do that). It's about a variable cost mentality that pervades Sam's life and much of his generation. It's a mentality that

many of us wish we had adopted long ago. Drop.io is
evolving into a true variable cost company.

Let's talk about what drop.io costs are not variable,
starting with its real estate. Interestingly, in my generation,
venture real estate was one of the few costs that could
have been variable. I was friends with Debra Larsen and
Bruce Bockmann (who was Morgan's most playful
partner, choosing once, when I was a young associate, to
introduce us to a new client with our roles reversed) who
created TechSpace and thus pioneered the concept of
monthly rental of venture space with centralized relevant
services. But Sam chose, in a rare instant, not to go with
variable cost. The reason is DUMBO.

DUMBO is one of the last largely undiscovered "cool"
locations in New York. DUMBO stands for "Down
Under the Manhattan Bridge Overpass" – leaving little
doubt of its location. The best use of his space, were it not
so well situated, would be a self storage facility. His
landlord, by playing quietly in the minor leagues, now
finds himself in the major league (it reminds me of
Jefferies – we find ourselves as one of the largest
independent investment banks, not just because we grew
so fast – although we did – but because our competitors
all shot themselves in the head). His monthly rental cost
for the next 3 years of cavernous space is $6500/month.
Variable cost is a terrific mentality except when the fixed
cost is so compelling. His space reminds me of Wit
Capital.

Drop.io's other fixed cost is development. I think of
promotion in terms of marketing and customer acquisition
costs. Sam thinks about exposing the blogs to your service
and letting their audience promote or pan it. With that
mentality, the one functionality you have to get right is
product development. Drop.io is programmed exclusively

in the most versatile and manipulable (i.e. lowest variable cost) programming language, Ruby on Rails.

That's it for fixed costs. Now let's discuss what's not.

For starters, the technological hardware costs. For a technology company, they own no hardware. In fact, other than flat screens and keyboards, there is no technology on-site.

Virtual memory has been an evolution since the commercialization of the Internet. It started with dedicated servers, located in the office of the web company. It was solely the responsibility of the company to maintain these servers and, when/if they grew, more servers would be purchased. Over time, co-location developed whereby servers would be housed in massive facilities that were equipped to handle the conditions of multiple users. The website would rent a footprint within that facility and purchase space as its needs grew. But memory was not really virtual – it was "lumpy" in that it could be added only in increments of a server. Days of forewarning were needed to add (it was difficult to subtract) capacity. "Cloud computing", which defines 100% of drop.io's needs, is 100% variable cost—the servers, which are all owned by Amazon (who initially had massive overcapacity from holiday periods), can be "virtually" added or subtracted on an hourly basis; you are renting memory by the hour! And you thought Amazon sold books.

It would not be true to say drop.io has no marketing expenses but nor would it be far off. To date, their success has been based on word of mouth which, leveraging the world's connectivity, is rapid and global. In fact, Sam questions the legitimacy of all unfocused advertising in a digitally connected society.

Within days of their launch, they were picked up by blogs around the world. Translating the multitude of languages into English (through Google translator), it became clear that privacy is a global concern. Much of their marketing is done by making available their source code (API's) to others, letting the users do all their customization. Sam's vision is that ultimately every internet service is seamlessly interconnected and the leading sites are merely jumping off points to begin the user's journey.

Drop.io has no secretaries. Sam's cell phone voice mail is connected to "Phonetag" which, powered by a mechanical turk, immediately accesses talent around the world to transcribe his voicemail into email. Not only are there no healthcare costs, there are no monthly costs for the next year as his service is a one year trial. When Sam doesn't return my voice messages, I know it's intentional.

He does travel extensively, both for business and for pleasure (remember how this section begins), but he runs his itinerary as a largely variable expense. When possible, he departs from Kennedy Airport; JFK is the last stop on the E train; if the MTA misprices its service by charging a single fare regardless of distance, Sam will capitalize on it. While his flight bookings are last minute, it is his lodging that defines his generation. Only upon landing at his destination will he then begin to contemplate where to sleep. To have made a commitment beforehand is likely suboptimal. Leveraging Google Maps on his Blackberry, he will cross reference his location with the best available lodging values at that time.

This is not an essay on how easy it is to live a productive life in New York City. Sam is well aware of how much my and Naida's relationships have helped him along the way. Sam is the beneficiary of a lot of fixed costs, starting with his education, incurred by his mom and me. One might argue that Sam's disregard for owning assets is a consequence of being surrounded by so many while growing up. I wonder, were my generation to lose its assets, whether his generation would devote itself to replenishing them. I'm also curious how much of Sam's variable mentality will survive once he has the responsibility of children.

I can't wait to spend quality adult time with my two younger children – Danny and Kara. I suspect that, when I do, there is much I will learn.

29. The key to venture capital investing is don't run out of cash. If you want to piss off attendees at a venture capital conference, explain to them that the key to venture investing is to not run out of money. At best they will feel like they wasted their time, at worst they will feel like they have wasted their time and their money. Having said that, it's true. As you approach the point of no cash, the death rattle (observation number 23) begins. The key is to raise capital and not dilute yourself too early or too late.

30. But raise enough cash to enable you to refine your business model. In Dawntreader, we own a meaningful stake in Greenplum, a very exciting company focused on efficient solutions for data warehousing. How did we get that? We started with Metapa. Which provided unifying digital formats for media companies, found out that we didn't have enough capital to pursue our vision, merged it into a parallel processing technology company called Didera, and changed the mission and the name (the latter thanks to the CEO's 7 year old daughter) to Greenplum. Our investment in HNW, the leader in interactive marketing solutions focused on the high net worth market, started as our investment in worth.com, a website that was the digital analogy to *Worth* Magazine.

The examples of dramatically restructured business plans are plentiful. The key is to acknowledge when a strategy is not working soon enough that you have enough capital to repurpose your plan. Like most aspects of life, it comes down to living without hubris.

31. Don't partner with those with whom you haven't gone through BAD times. Sometime after Wit and before Jefferies I thought about establishing a venture firm with David Beirne. David, who was then the head of Ramsey Beirne (the premier technology recruiter), and I represented an ideal combination, on paper. Having said that, we had never worked together.

It didn't take us long to figure out that we truly did not like each other. Fortunately, no money was ever raised.

Not surprisingly, one of the attributes an investor looks at as part of their "due diligence" in deciding whether to invest in a fund, is how long has the partnership been together – shotgun relationships, no matter how theoretically appealing, simply are too risky.

SIX

MY STROKE

L ess than a year into my leadership of Smith Barney, I was felled by a stroke. I'm told it was one of the more serious strokes the doctors had seen.

In an exercise of unanticipated consequences, my stroke was probably caused by the then inexact radiation when treating my Hodgkin's - which itself was possibly (my theory) caused by a blood disorder from, what turned out to be, tainted drinking water.

For thirteen hours I lay deteriorating in bed at home, with an unengaged general practitioner telephonically assuring Naida that I was surely "suffering" from a severe ear infection. Ultimately her Dad, who is a well known neurologist, arrived; his decision was whether to admit me to Englewood Hospital, which was 5 minutes away, or Columbia Presbyterian, where he was then head doctor, which was ten minutes. Thankfully, he chose the latter.

I was hospitalized for two months. I was unable to either walk or eat for a year. My first meal, when I was allowed to eat, was a Big Mac; I do regret missing the promotional opportunity.

So what did I learn from the stroke?

32. Try to experience a major setback every decade. If you aren't dealt one, create one. Get yourself fired. Get seriously sick. Get divorced. If you don't, you'll end up with way too many friends. You'll end life not knowing who your friends really are. You'll be amazed, when you have a setback, how few friends you really have. But those will be true friends. And the list will grow until your next setback. You will end life with a collection of true friends.

When I had my stroke, most of the people I knew on Wall Street were indifferent to whether I returned. Some actively hoped I wouldn't. I have a pretty good sense of how people behaved; I doubt that I'll forget.

33. When physically compromised, remain mentally engaged. When I had Hodgkin's I worked tirelessly on the Marsh Mac deal. The day after I was hospitalized with my stroke, Naida was by my side asking me to opine on various investment banking decisions. I responded as best I could with a thumb up or down. I later learned that all the issues were fictitious. The division was functioning just fine without me. Naida knew to keep me cognitively engaged. Later in my recovery I did solicit real clients with real mandates. I was quite effective in obtaining secondary roles; no one really wants to turn down a stroke victim.

34. While doctors might determine your survival, nurses determine your recovery. I don't doubt that my survival is a result of living near one of the great medical teaching hospitals; I was treated by a renowned team of physicians with cutting edge techniques that, even a year before, were unavailable. But, equally, I don't doubt that my recovery was a result of gifted nursing. After two weeks in the ER, I was moved to the McKeon Pavilion on the condition that I hire round the clock nursing. With its high tea and daily piano performances, it is the five star analogy to hospital care. It also does nothing for a patient who cannot eat, move, nor leave their room. My entertainment was not a concert pianist, but a Billy Ray Cyrus CD that played non-stop; no one will ever get me to badmouth Miley. Ironically, unbeknownst to us, my current senior assistant, Sandy, who has become my closest confidante, was then hospitalized herself a few rooms away. But after a month I was moved to a ward which, I was told, would offer me my one chance of independent recovery.

From the absence of a donor name alone, it is clear that there is nothing appealing about the Neurological Center. I was greeted with no warmth and told, indifferently, to infuse my medicine. Maybe the nurse was unaware that I just had a stroke. My initial attempts to follow her demands were futile. But ultimately I would learn to regain a modicum of independence, the independence that I would need to depart permanent care.

I'm apt to run into my doctors. They are intrigued by my recovery and we travel in somewhat connected circles. I'm sorry that I don't have the privilege of again meeting my nurses.

35. It's the ones closest to the patient that suffer most. It should be comforting to know that it is the patient, not the loved ones, who suffer least. When you are the patient, you are in the "zone". You are focused on your next breath. With triple pneumonia, I was intubated for what seemed to be an interminable period. The breathing tube would be removed only when my pulse, which was displayed real time, would drop below a certain level. I knew that number; that alone, is what I focused on.

36. Reconnecting with your children is the overriding motivation to recover. Naida, in her wisdom, determined that our three young children would not be visiting me in the hospital. She did not want them seeing me unable to move and fully wired with monitors. Their absence was a determining motivation to leave.

As a doctor's daughter, she knew that patients are stabilized, but don't recover, in hospitals. She repurposed our home with ramps so that I might return. It would be many months before I could walk. My eldest son embraced my limitations while my just born daughter enjoyed them; I fear that the condition of my return, at a very delicate age, may have had a lasting impact on my middle child.

I witnessed many elderly patients with no visitors and no one to come home to. They often died in the hospital.

37. Strength comes from unexpected sources. I am a huge believer in unintended consequences, both positive and negative. Who would have thought that the comfort that I developed with the elderly, through my college dancing at Arthur Murray, would put me at ease in the geriatric populated stroke ward?

38. There is great satisfaction in playing a tough hand well. My favorite movie, even more than *Forrest Gump,* is *The Diving Bell and the Butterfly* is about Jean-Dominique Bauby, the editor of *Elle* magazine, who claws his way back after being felled by a stroke. Most of my friends find it depressing. I find it incredibly uplifting.

Having said that, please don't give too much credit to either Mr. Bauby or me. Our brain, independent of our effort, often does an amazing job of rewiring itself. When I first showered after my stroke, each side of my body felt distinctly different temperatures; I had no idea whether I was stepping into a freezing or scalding shower. Now, without thinking, the erroneous temperature is discarded. I was not allowed to eat after the stroke for fear of asphyxiation; my esophagus is still paralyzed but, subconsciously, I know that I now swallow on my functioning side. I had to relearn tennis with two handed strokes, each hand signaling a different position relative to the ball. Now the erroneous signal is automatically discarded—I miss balls because I stink.

39. Pain is a critical early warning system. I thought the one "silver lining" of a stroke is that one side of the body feels no pain. Until I learned of my hand burning by the charred smell of its flesh, that is. I now understand that pain is a necessary warning mechanism. I expect that I will ultimately perish by suffering internal injuries on my side that feels nothing. I do, however, insist, as a rare benefit to an absence of pain, that the nurses draw blood from my left finger.

40. Find irony and humor in the most challenging of circumstances. I doubt that you can find humor, other than the most macabre, in a serious stroke. I can. I was cared for by a Filipino nurse, one of the most beautiful women that I have ever encountered. One day, while she was dressing me, my right hand, the stroke impacted side, brushed by her left breast. "Don't worry," I assured her, "this side feels nothing but", I continued, "if it ever can, you will be the <u>last</u> to know!"

On a less sexual note, I shared an approximate stroke date with Saul Steinberg. Soon, after we were both released, he invited me over to an exquisite lunch at his luxurious apartment. His chef served us… spaghetti. Try to imagine two newly released stroke victims eating their plates of spaghetti. An opportunity for a classic scene in a hysterical film was lost.

I maintain a daily diary. Most of my entries ("today, I walked the dog") are of no interest to anyone, myself included. But I use it also to record the most awkward and annoying events and thus I find a basis for relishing them. How many others have looked forward to their car being impounded by the NYC Police Department?

Last month I was analyzed, more than 16 years after the stroke, so that the doctors could better understand my recovery. I am claustrophobic. I hate MRI's. I vowed that I would never consciously undergo one again. But, when I demurred, they explained that, as one of the best recoveries they had seen, they want to understand better how my brain had rewired itself.

This may or may not be true. It may be a telemarketer who was instructed, if the patient hesitates, tell them he's had the best recovery ever. Whatever. At least I drafted a compelling journal entry.

SEVEN

NON VENTURE INVESTING

My non venture investments, which are every bit as vast as my venture investments, are equally unsuccessful. Through these investments, I have learned much to be imparted.

41. Business is best understood as a collection of feedback loops. Each year, at the end of the semester, I try to distill for my 7th and 8th grade students the principles we learned in our year's study of world events. None is more compelling, in my mind, than our study of feedback loops. Each event has its probability weighted implications that, ultimately, will feed back upon the event itself.

Our most complex feedback loop starts with an incremental unemployed individual and, by the end of the class, fills the entire blackboard. No one can convince me that we are recovering so long as we are still losing employees.

42. No transaction stands alone. My contribution to Wall Street was analyzing each transaction with the mentality that no transaction stands by itself. Every deal has implications. Obviously competitors are affected but so too are customers and suppliers. The key to creating transactions is to analyze each deal with this perspective.

43. Investing is all about identifying the second and third order implications of an event. The direct impact of a transaction is quickly understood and priced immediately into the market. It is the next orders of transaction implications that take longer to comprehend and require human insight. And it is by anticipating these that investors can outperform in an otherwise largely efficient market.

44. The difference between good and great is hugely disproportionate with the underlying value. This, regretfully, is a theory, not just of investing, but of life. The difference between superior and excellent commands a premium that is unjustified by performance. This is partially because of feedback loops and partially because the world has so much capital interested only in the absolute best.

Mostly "superior" pricing is justified because it maintains its values. Examples would include real estate in the Hamptons or major league baseball salaries. But there are examples of the converse such as my family living in the worst neighborhoods of the best towns – garnering the same quality education as my wealthier cohabitants.

45. With regard to real estate, the worst case scenario is apt to happen. I have learned this the hard way. If zoning allows, a parking garage will be built next to your bucolic property. If zoning does not allow it, it someday will. The only protected real estate is bounded by ocean or national forest. Otherwise, always, if possible, buy contiguous property. Certainly avoid Beijing, Dubai, or Miami Beach apartments (two of the three of which I actually managed to avoid) – demand will never be allowed to equal supply.

46. Black swans. Nassim Nicholas Taleb does a great job describing the "Black Swan" theory – that mankind is poorly equipped to comprehend, and thus misprices, outlying probabilities (there, I saved you the time to read his book).

Recently, our Ambassador was recounting to a group of us the ethical missteps of an individual from one of the world's more unstable geographies. My guest reacted with disgust, asking whether this individual has been imprisoned. "Oh no," replied our Ambassador. "He will be the country's next President."

We can't ignore the reality that most of our world's leaders are, or very soon will be, new to the world stage. Inexperience combined with instantaneous communications make Black Swans.

47. Round numbers are arbitrary and misleading. It is an incomprehensible human shortcoming that we gravitate to round numbers (the Dow may break 10,000 again) or historical precedents. So what – it's a number. Who picked base 10 anyway? The only time that a specific number seems to matter is when it is of a medical result that determines the course of your treatment (like whether your pulse is at a level for the doctor to feel comfortable removing your breathing tube).

48. Think of diversification holistically. When I think of my greatest mistakes, a title for which there is massive competition, one of the greatest had to be owning financial stocks while being paid by the financial industry.

My leaving Morgan Stanley to join Smith Barney was not all about personal loyalty. It was also about money. I was offered a direct participation in Smith Barney's investment banking profits. The percentage was not small, and, when Smith Barney employees learned of this, neither was their reaction. As an act of reconciliation, I agreed to take all my compensation in Primerica (ultimately Citibank) stock. I thought I had the last laugh when the stock went from $7 to $55; I didn't when it later went to $2. My outsized compensation, had, in the end, turned out to be quite modest.

In fairness, it was not greed that motivated my reluctance to sell my Citigroup stock. The basis of the stock was low and thus the stock was best used for charitable gifts (I was well on my way to giving it away). Also, in fairness, half the stock had been given up in my divorce and Naida, in her wisdom, had zero interest in holding anything owned by me.

But the loss still stung. And I now ask myself how could I consider myself diversified when my major source of income (Jefferies) is dependent on the health of the financial industry? Think of diversification in a holistic mindset.

EIGHT

JEFFERIES

I joined Jefferies in the fall of 2002. Out of a combination of laziness and arrogance, I had missed my chance to join at an even more favorable time when I failed to show up at a meeting where they were interested in buying Wit SoundView. They interpreted my absence, probably rightly so, as an expression of indifference.

But it compelled me to watch this company more closely, a company whose namesake and origin, unlike Morgan Stanley, had a pretty non illustrious past (for starters, I had never worked at an established firm that had only one name).

I visited the CEO, Rich Handler, and was incredibly impressed by much, most notably his attire that was even more casual than mine. This was my type of firm; I told Rich that I would start immediately. This was a bit disorienting to him; he had not decided whether to make me an offer.

I needed to come up with a rationale (other than professional failure) of how a leading Morgan Stanley banker had ended up at Jefferies. Less elegant, and less expensive, than Nike's "Just Do It", my tag line was that "Jefferies – the last great build up on Wall Street"; it appears now that it is.

49. I'm not creative enough to retire. Consistent with many philosophies, including the need to lose friends and recharge, I did retire briefly after my departure from Wit. My focus was on tennis. Stroke-affected, no one had ever worked so hard to be so mediocre at an activity. I equated my tennis performance to that of a dyslexic at a spelling bee. Since the stroke, I have played only with instructors, a number of whom lived with me, who are able to place the ball with such precision that, unless I want to, I never need to run. As I've often said, "I don't play with those I don't pay."

But playing tennis and retiring are two very different mindsets. While I no longer awoke at 3am, I still always wake before the sun rises. I would read the three relevant newspapers (starting with the *NY Post* which, at its best, is a substitute for coffee), and, when it was once appropriate, take a child to school. My first "appointment" was tennis at 11 am.

I would play twice per day for many reasons, including the fact that, with the property tax I was paying, playing twice a day and hitting only forehands, came to one dollar per forehand; I had to amortize the court.

But it was only 8:30am. Tennis was not for another 2.5 hours. I could play only so much solitaire. When my non-English speaking housecleaner became my best friend, I knew it was time to get a job.

50. There is a real cost of arrogance. For someone who believes that the main skill of an investment banker is "to show up", it's quite amazing that I failed to do so when the management of Jefferies asked to meet with the management of Wit SoundView. This was not, after all, a Mideast peace treaty where the details have to be worked out before the leaders arrive. And, it's not as if I believe in physical meetings more than once.

But I didn't show up, maybe because my Morgan training had taught me never even to spell Smith Barney let alone Jefferies.

Jefferies has a pretty sharp pencil; I don't know if they would have paid more for Wit than what Schwab ultimately paid. But my arrogance cost me two years of inevitable employment.

So why is it that Jefferies is the last great build up on Wall Street? It's partially because the firm's origins are in trading to which it ultimately added an investment bank. Great firms need both disciplines. But it's impossible to build a real trading operation around a bank. Jefferies, inadvertently, got the order right.

The second reason is because we have a CEO who actually likes details. He still trades actively on behalf of Jefferies and its clients and understands, on a real time basis, the markets as well as anyone alive. Most CEO's, I once included, have long since lost interest in details.

51. Don't minimize the importance of permanent capital. But what makes Jefferies most unique is its CEO's paranoia. He would not have known that the best event that he ever experienced was being a young employee of Drexel Burnham when it imploded. Speaking of unintended consequences, it taught Rich the importance of always being well capitalized in the financial community.

He raised long term debt when it was priced like cheap equity. He raised equity that others rejected as unnecessarily dilutive. And when the crisis hit, we were the least levered major firm on Wall Street.

We hired first class talent with abandon – offering our new employees a chance to be paid what they were worth, not what the government said they were. And we allowed them to function in an environment with minimal political distraction.

In the year of the credit crisis we hired 500 new employees (out of a total of 2300) as the rest of industry was actively disgorging its talent.

52. Surround yourself with your complement. Jefferies is marching toward greatness under the leadership of not one, but two leaders – Rich and Brian Friedman. On the surface, they couldn't be more different. Rich is as intuitive as Brian is analytical. Brian wears a tailored suit while Rich wears jeans. Brian's office is reflective of his stature while Rich works out of what looks to be a cleaner's closet. But they work together seamlessly and without agenda. It gives the rest of us a choice of which leader to introduce – based on the peculiarities of our client. It reminds me of Mike and me when we ran the bank at Smith Barney. Every firm, at least in the service industry, should have two leaders – if they are too similar, they should chose amongst themselves which divergent aura they will project.

Maybe corporate America should not so resist political pressures to disaggregate the Chairman from the Chief Executive.

NINE

GENERAL OBSERVATIONS ON INVESTMENT BANKING

I am now well into my 33rd year on Wall Street. I started sufficiently young that my shelf life has not yet (I believe) expired. So what have I learned independent of specific firms? I would suggest the key lessons are as follows:

53. My best professional skill is showing up on time. To show up late for a meeting is an unambiguous statement of arrogance – that, "My time is more valuable than yours." I will never show up late; it's impossible to dig out from this subliminal insult.

What's nearly as rude as being late is speaking to clients on your speaker phone. The subliminal message is that your client is not significant enough to warrant your picking up the phone. And that their insights are not privileged enough to restrict. When bankers converse on speakerphones with their doors open, it exceeds tardy meetings in rudeness. The message is now, "Everyone listen to my call, which is so much more interesting than yours". I much prefer street sounds to those of a banker. It makes not physically showing up to work even more compelling.

54. I enter each meeting with the objective of leaving with answers to just a handful of specific questions. If you never show up late, you have to be able to condense a meeting into its essence. A one hour meeting might need to be conducted in 5 minutes; I can do this without losing effectiveness. The key is to anticipate the handful of questions for which you want answers. Sometimes I forewarn the client that I have this focused agenda. Sometimes, I start with the statement, "If I could have an answer to only one question it would be...." I rarely care how his kids are doing anyway.

55. I run meetings in 15 minute segments. Consistent with the arbitrariness of round numbers, I have no respect for the magic of an hour. My meeting's "scripts" are written in 15 minute segments. I am four times more effective, or four times lazier, than most everyone else on Wall Street.

It reminds me of my one, and only, experience speed dating. We had one trial run; when asked at the end of the seven minutes whether we had any questions, I raised my hand to ask, "What do I do with the other six minutes?"

Ironically, given the declining cost of memory and bandwidth, there is an increasing premium on tighter communications. Phone conversations evolve into e-mail which evolves into texting which evolves into tweets. I never forget that The Gettysburg Address is America's finest speech.

One of the benefits of this book is that I get to tighten my own communication. I now can convey observations by uttering a number. I've disgorged everything that I now know and have only a few incremental insights. It reminds me of my father's favorite joke.

The comedians in the Catskills are so repetitive that they evolve ultimately, not to telling jokes, but to numbering their jokes and simply reciting the numbers to the audience, which is equally well trained and responds with uncontrollable laughter. One day a young comedian's numerical performance is met with total silence. "What happened?" he asks his more seasoned colleague when he gets backstage. He responds with disgust, "You told it wrong."

56. I dictate the contents of the meeting immediately after it's accomplished. As soon as I complete a meeting, I dictate its contents. I circulate the news and it evokes suggestions from around the Investment Bank. Just as important, all clients are impressed when you recount the content of the last meeting, as if you have had no meetings since then. As if I'm not 54!

57. Walking between meetings leverages the appeal of New York City. New York City is irreplaceable for many reasons but one is that it is the ultimate walking city. Some genius town planner put New York streets into a grid format and thus made every address identifiable. 200 years later, we have the technology that embraces complete mobility. I walk because it's healthy. I walk because I observe – I watch the vacancies arise and think through the implications. And I walk because everyone else does – it creates chance encounters with relationships you would otherwise forget. Manhattan is a geography of serendipity.

58. I begin relationships with a physical meeting with the expectation that thereafter they are apt to be electronic. There is no substitute for a first physical meeting. There is a trust that arises from sharing DNA that is, as of yet, irreplaceable with technology. In fact, I judge the quality of a coverage officer's relationships by how he (this is a "he" issue) is greeted when meeting a client; a "man hug" tells me that there is a real relationship But having done so, it is equally clear to me that, until another milestone is reached, there is no need for another physical meeting. Most people prefer to correspond by email; I don't recall when I last heard a voicemail – particularly since a globally outsourced service, Phonetag, converts mine into email.

59. The only better answer than "I don't know" is "I don't know and I'll find out." I don't recall ever being disrespected for admitting that I don't know an answer. I would be disrespectful if I didn't then take the time to find it out.

60. A misrepresentation when caught (which it inevitably will be) begs the inevitable question of what other lies have you told me that I haven't yet figured out. I don't now know anyone that lies. Our environment is too interconnected. If ever caught, it would discredit all future statements. None of us have the time to sort through half-truths.

61. Business is an excuse to stay in touch with friends. I'm asked why I still work. There are two answers. First, have you ever seen my property tax bill? Second, business is an excuse to stay in touch with my friends. When I'm not working, I will ask about a friend's children. Six months later I will ask and learn that the children are still fine. It reminds me of my socially connected British friend. Prince Charles dropped by and asked about my friend's Dad, only to learn that he had died. Six months later Prince Charles met my friend again and, subliminally equating him with his dad, again asked about his dad. He replied, "Still dead." With business, I use the volatility of the markets, whether I ultimately discuss them or not, as an excuse to stay in touch with my friends.

62. I live in a world of two degrees of separation.
Sorry John Gaure, I don't live in a world of six degrees of separation. Everyone I know, or want to get to know, is separated by one friend. The challenge is to identify that connection.

63. Investment banking is great when devoid of politics.
It took eight years but no one thinks that I have any agenda to rise organizationally within Jefferies. I have the Vice Chairman title that I always wanted. I have run three investment banks. Running an investment bank is a title that you want only long enough to put on your resume.

I view all my conversations as belonging to Jefferies and thus share them liberally. I get input throughout the bank with unanticipated ideas. I am not bothered with who takes credit for anything. I propose to the Firm ideas that are noted and then likely ignored.

Investment banking, under the right circumstances, is a very appealing life.

TEN

THE CREDIT CRISIS

We all just lived through the most incredible credit crisis. What made it incredible was first that there was no place to hide. Everything I owned, from Russian equity to Chinese property, declined 60% in value. Second, there was a direct correlation between sophistication and carnage. With the low cost of debt, I believed it to be irresponsible NOT to incur some leverage – 60% declines became 70%.

So what did I learn that can be passed on to, and likely ignored by, future generations?

64. We forgot that expected returns are a function of risk AND liquidity. Theoretically, returns align with risk

AND LIQUIDITY. We forgot the latter. Actually, we are pretty good at envisioning the risk; but we were totally blinded by illiquidity. We all had our hedge fund investments with quarterly liquidity; we never envisioned that they would all break the "social contract" and deprive us of our capital by "putting up their gates". And without liquidity, there is no reasonable return that can justify the risk.

65. The skills of running a company in a capital constrained world align very well with venture capital.
As a venture investor, I found the crisis surprisingly not disorienting. A credit crisis restructures priorities from profits to cash. This is the mandate of venture capital; it was not particularly confusing.

66. To survive a capital crisis is, ultimately, to thrive.
Jefferies is a prime example. On a lesser scale, so too is iParty. iParty, of which I own 40%, is the leading New England retailer of party goods (it is, in fairness, a small company – think "smartest utility executive"). It is largely, but not totally, immune to the recession – you may not shop at Saks but are you really going to deprive your children of their two year old birthday? The crisis is a rare opportunity to renegotiate leases and acquire smaller stores that are not capitalized to withstand the downturn.

67. A world of transactional opportunity becomes available when transactions are stripped of ego. In normal times, the human agenda is such that there is a vast difference between what should happen and what will happen. Ego is stripped away in times of crisis; what should and will happen are apt to converge.

68. Unemployment, on the way up, is evolving from a lagging indicator to a leading indicator. Companies increasingly run their cost structures with a real time sensitivity to the business environment. They enter the year with "Plan A" but have in their back pocket "Plan B". Employment used to await confirmation of a downturn; it is now much more anticipatory. Yet, on the way down, unemployment remains a lagging indicator. Employers are reluctant to add workers or space. Employment has become the worst of both worlds.

69. The talent once sucked up by Wall Street will find entrepreneurial endeavors. Watching us all curtail our school hiring efforts, I was initially saddened for the graduates who found that they had missed the hiring window by one year (it reminds me of a Morgan Stanley colleague who, having been married in 1968, noted one alcohol infested night that "mankind had waited ten thousand years for the sexual revolution and I missed it by one year").

But I soon realized that the talent that we once absorbed is now engaged with starting venture companies. The cost of technology is such that starting a company requires one or two zeroes fewer than when I was active. Our banking missteps have engendered a generation of budding entrepreneurs.

70. Pursue your passion. When I was graduating from college, a number of my friends entered medicine for no reason other than its alleged financial security. What an incredible miscalculation. The same goes for investment banking. The odds are not trivial that you will be terminated along the way; before you have generated financial security but after you have incurred a high fixed cost structure, the markets are apt to hit a bump and you may be let go. When our industry again hires, it rarely looks back.

With all the recent fury over investment **banker** compensation, the public is disinclined to understand that the recipients are the survivors—so many talented professionals have been asked to leave along the way. For those remaining, small differences in skill result in enormous differences in remuneration. How is this different than professional sports? Athletes aren't disgorged when the economy turns down.

Residing with us until he finds his footing is a young Wall Street professional of incredible talent who found himself in the wrong place at the wrong time. A decade ago he came to our country with no obvious skill, other than, as one of the world's best tennis players, an uncanny ability to hit a moving object. Within eight years, he learns English, graduates from MIT in electrical engineering and computer science, graduates from Harvard Business School, becomes a US citizen and lands a job at one of the most prestigious Wall Street firms. Who says that there isn't phenomenal talent on Wall Street.

He now waits for his next employer's phone call that, as of yet, has not come. I wish those that have kept their jobs could better envision the lives of those who have not; a little decency would result in a lifetime of loyalty.

Whatever you personally endeavor, the only antidote for financial insecurity is passion.

ELEVEN

HAPPINESS

All observations until now are irrelevant without a distillation of what I have learned about happiness. As this is a personal journal, much, but not all of it, presupposes a certain economic comfort. But, with that caveat, here it is.

71. Outsource life's details to the few that you trust. I am blessed with two personal assistants who are more talented than I; when the issue involves my life and not theirs, they are able to emotionally disassociate themselves from the issue.

My senior assistant, Sandy, is certainly more insightful and more credentialed than I. I wanted very much to invest in a friend's fund but, upon reading the offering document she informed me that this was irresponsible. I explained to her that I had no choice as the General Partner was my friend. She asked if I knew how to wire money. When I told her that, of course, I didn't, she concluded our conversation by saying, "Then I guess we aren't going to invest, are we?"

I can focus on writing stupid books.

72. Don't bother to know what you can't change. I receive a call from Eric, my terrific tax accountant, "Can we discuss your estimated third quarter taxes?" "Eric," I ask, "can I change them?" "No." "Then why", I question, "would you ruin my day?"

73. Focus on your own happiness and don't be affected by the happiness of others. One of the greatest burdens is to compare your happiness to others. There must be few curses worse than wanting to be the world's richest person. It's been noted what a good life my Cyprus staff must live for the ten months that I'm not there; that's great, but I'm focused on the two months that I am.

74. You really are as happy as your least happy child. A well travelled observation that is too true not to observe; I don't even pretend that there is a disconnect – I will call my children and ask them how <u>my</u> day was today.

75. There is no happiness without human contact. I have a love/hate relationship with human contact. When first exposed to the Internet, I used it as an experiment to see how disconnected from people I could be. It was intellectually intriguing and emotionally disastrous.

Once I bought my Kindle, I realized there would no longer be a need to visit my bagel store at 5am to pick up the newspapers. This worked well for quite awhile except I realized how much I missed their early morning greetings. Last month I went to the bagel store and asked them how much they would charge me if I just cared to buy the "good morning".

But human contact, at least with me, does not necessarily presume a compelling environment. It is no secret that I serve the most unappealing lunches on Wall Street. Rarely are my sandwiches consumed; that's okay, tomorrow's sandwich, at least for me, is apt to be the uneaten portion of today's. It reminds me of Linda Wachner, the ex-CEO of Warnaco, who claimed to me that, once so poor, she ate her half sandwich in front of a mirror so that the reflection would trick her into believing she was eating and entire sandwich.

When my guests insist on eating lunch out, I will suggest my new favorite restaurant in Long Island City. While incredibly convenient (one subway stop) it sounds both inconvenient and slightly dangerous. Many of my guests end up cancelling.

It's not that I'm necessarily opposed to a nice setting; I just want to spend time with guests who are interested in spending time with me independent of their perceived trappings of my environment.

76. There is a vast difference between great and perfect connectivity. With few joys greater than wandering, I can do so only with perfect connectivity.

The common mentality of a Wall Street professional is a sense of perishability. Opportunities avail themselves with no forewarning and evaporate as quickly as they appeared.

To be well, but not perfectly, (wirelessly) connected is to engender guilt that overwhelms the sense of freedom. The New York City subway system would benefit from a massive increase in ridership if all its routes, like those of many other countries, had mobile connectivity.

I never understood those few friends who fear having permanent access to information. My access is a call option on information, not a requirement.

77. When your career can handle it, establish a reputation for sartorial indifference. Mostly out of cheapness, long ago I established a reputation disconnected from my attire. In fact, it was very connected – inversely so.

It evolved consistently throughout my established career (the knot of my tie descended throughout my days at Morgan Stanley) until the formality of my attire took a quantum leap backwards when I took Tommy Hilfiger public.

But, even more so than Tommy Hilfiger, the high (or low, depending on how you look at it) point of my sartorial taste had to be when I, on behalf of Smith Barney, was pitching to be part of the General Magic IPO.

General Magic was certainly one the hottest companies ever to grace the technology world. In direct contrast, Smith Barney was a past tense bank who had no right to be in the same town as General Magic. Marc Porat's (General Magic's CEO) sister was a dear colleague but she could do no more than get us a hearing.

My presentation to Marc was going as well as could be expected – i.e. nowhere. In desperation, I put all my cards on the table and exclaimed, "Look Marc, I'll give you the shirt off my back to be in this deal." "Prove it" he responded.

With no hesitation I took off my shirt, gave it to him and continued my presentation shirtless.

Silicon Valley conference rooms are always glass enclosed. I don't know how passers-by viewed our ongoing dialogue with me flipping through a presentation appearing to be naked. They must have been even more surprised when we were included in the offering.

A few months after that, with great fanfare, the company went public. A year after that, the company was bankrupt. (Marc has since become a "national treasure" in understanding, and seeking to address, the challenges of the environment.)

The dot.com boom gave me the perfect opportunity to dress with indifference; no one ever told me that the sartorial bubble had burst. I would now be presumed to be looking for a job if I ever wore a suit (putting aside India and various Gulf countries for whom casual attire would be insulting).

I will admit that, even in this progressed stage of my career, my attire does result in occasional episodes of awkwardness. Last week, while waiting for a street light to change, a kind man places a quarter in my freshly ordered cup of Dunkin Donuts coffee.

My attire is now totally based on mobility. I need attire to accommodate my wireless devices. I need my "pouch" to hold all my relevant belongings – I could leave on no notice for Sri Lanka.

After months of looking, my partner, Clara, found me an additional pouch that carried my Kindle; it hooks onto my belt and, importantly for a stroke victim, balances my weight. But it's not an ideal situation. I now don't fit comfortably into airplane seats and spill over into my, often not amused, neighbor's space when riding the subway.

I never check a bag, regardless for how long I travel, and took a perverse pleasure when the airlines began charging for doing so. But I can't, with my dual pouches, close my seatbelt, in an airplane or a car.

At my best, I look like a digital nomad; at my worst I look like a homeless man compelled to carry his life's belongings. The latter is why, I suspect, my pouches have never caught on. Some fashion designer will figure out how to reconcile portability with taste.

Besides the aesthetic appeal, nomadic clothing lacks just one functionality – a charging capability. I'm tired of ordering an overpriced Starbucks coffee with the sole objective of charging my phone (Dunkin Donuts doesn't have chargers). The JUICY logo should be made of solar panels.

78. You can't have serendipity without human interaction. From one of my lesser satisfying relationships, I met the Cypriot friend of a woman I was seeing. Not only has he turned out to be one of my best friends but I now have the privilege of intimacy with his entire family. It's through their family that I now own a home on the coast of Cyprus to which I may ultimately retire. I would not have guessed this from what turned out to be an otherwise disappointing romantic relationship.

I hosted my 50th birthday party in Barbados. The 150 friends who attended will confirm that it was a defining celebration from many perspectives.

But it was those who were not in attendance that had most impacted my life. Of course I thought first of my twin brother who was too ill to travel. I thought of the air traveler across the aisle from me who once dislodged the steak from my throat, undoubtedly saving my life. I thought of the doctor who visited the hospital on his day off to suck the phlegm from my lungs. These people affected me more than anyone, yet I never saw them again.

79. Don't rely entirely on technology. "I'm packing and leaving you" Clara exclaims when I finally reach her last week. I'm confused. I know that I've not been a perfect boyfriend, but I'm pretty good, especially compared to how I was dismissively characterized recently by a young, unsuccessful (I believe) suitor of Clara's as "that middle-aged Jew from New Jersey". I learn, ultimately, that my report of my medical success has been mistranslated (by Phonetag) into a more incriminating message. "Hey Babe, it was great…" has been translated into:

Subject: Phonetag from Bob Cell
To: Clara email
Date: Thursday, September 24, 2009, 9:10AM
Hey Jade, it's me everyone craves. I called your home, you weren't there. Jenine just called but just let you know it was great. Thanks baby. Bye.

I must admit, it does feel pretty juicy. It reads as if I'm having a threesome with both Jade and Janine; I'm gracious, arrogant and self-congratulatory.

Somewhere in the world, someone from a developing country is spending their day translating Western voicemails into emails. I sincerely hope that this is more than human error, mine or theirs. I hope that it's the craftsmanship of a creative worker who, partially out of boredom, is intrigued by the idea of changing a word here or there and, in doing so, fundamentally changing a Westerner's life. If so, I would like to meet him someday and take him out to dinner.

Technological breakdowns don't have to be as dramatic as the jamming of Gmail or Twitter, both of which happened this summer, or Russia paralyzing Estonia's Internet, which happened last summer. Having said that, Clara is continually on the lookout for a Jade or a Janine. I, in turn, might consider again taking dancing lessons. Then again, as the young generation has commandeered ballroom dancing, it looks like I've waited 35 years to again be generationally inappropriate.

80. Date outside your culture. On the premise that it is a remote possibility that any relationship will be lasting, the fundamental question should be what lasting impact can I obtain from a relationship? Americans are embarrassingly insular. I can think of nothing more lasting than leveraging a relationship to learn about another culture.

During one of my periods of unemployment, I agreed with my partner that every two weeks we would meet anywhere in the world as long as the location is between us. She then lived in Hong Kong; technically, everywhere in the world was between us. She was quite flexible on the definition of "between us". In two months, we met three times in Buenos Aires (the Argentine Peso was then in freefall – having visited Sri Lanka, Myanmar and living in Northern Cyprus, we gravitate to countries with political turmoil). To get there she needed three connections and 28 hours of consecutive flying; I, in turn, took a fourteen hour nap. You can fall asleep on a plane in New York and wake up the next day most anywhere in the world.

81. Observe an illegal immigrant's sacrifice for their children. If you want to see sacrifice, watch the illegal immigrant community. I love massage (it almost achieved its own heading under "Happiness" until I realized that my kids might be reading this) and find that most of the New York masseuses are highly educated Asians. Without a social security number they are unable to find US employment consistent with their skills. Their gifted children may well not be allowed to attend university. And their sacrifice is for no reason other than to better the economic condition of their families. Let's put carrying your skis under a ski lift in perspective. I do hope that President Obama has not used up all his political goodwill over healthcare.

82. Don't over-negotiate. I learned this first when I "hit the bid" from Morgan Stanley but have learned subsequently, both positively and negatively, so many times. Negatively, I missed buying my dream home in Punta Del Este when my Argentine friends over-negotiated the deal. They were just trying to protect me but I have found that locals in their own country are apt, out of fondness, to over-negotiate. Positively, when I was getting divorced, Naida and I had a very clear idea of how we wanted to divide our assets. We endeavored, by choosing randomly from the local Yellow Pages, to find the two least aggressive New Jersey lawyers. Unfortunately, I did.

83. One's only lasting legacy comes from imparting insights. For several years now, I have had the privilege, and it really is a privilege, to teach New York City's brightest and poorest students. I teach "world events" and, as such, the world writes my weekly class notes. The year's events can be summarized into three buckets— every debate has two sides (I make the students argue the side that they don't believe in first); unintended consequences (we fight with the Mujahedeen and create Al Qaeda; George Bush mishandles nearly everything and, in doing so with energy, spikes oil and drives enormous investment into alternative energy); and feedback loops.

With the world writing my syllabus it sounds easy. Have you ever tried teaching Myanmar to kids who have never left New York? Have you ever tried teaching the credit crisis to smart eighth graders? Fortunately, I've lost significant wealth in the credit crisis and I've been to Myanmar.

I was a bit insulted when it was suggested that I teach eighth graders; I would now not teach anyone else – they are inquisitive and impressionable without ulterior motives (such as college recommendations). And, if it works the way it's supposed to, they too will ultimately teach others with exponential affect.

I contributed enough to Harvard that they offered to name a lecture hall after Naida and me. I chose a room in the computer center, partially because it resonated with me and largely because it was housed in a building newly constructed by a contribution from Bill Gates and Steve Ballmer. This would be the last building that Harvard would tear down.

For me, the naming was an emblem of pride, a confirmation of the American Dream. In one generation of good luck and hard work, I would be permanently recognized in the same geography where, as a young man, I once had felt so humbled. But for Sam, this recognition would be met with indifference; he, like all my children, would be forging his own identity.

When it comes to legacy I am not confused between edifice and education.

84. Don't equate assets with happiness. The problem is that my generation was trained to believe that accumulating assets was a hallmark of success. And with these assets come liabilities which, if they compel the sale of an asset, will do so exactly when it is unsalable. My friends have their planes, they have their boats – the expenses to maintain, let alone use, these assets are enormous and there is no way out. One dear friend, who is quite well off, reviewed his fixed operating expenses of supporting others, concluding, in the end, that he alone is the variable expense. Colleagues think it's great that I have an indoor tennis court until I tell them about my property tax.

It didn't start this way. But the States and municipalities, increasingly short of revenues, kept increasing local taxes. The Federal Government instituted AMT which eliminated the long history of deductibility of different jurisdictional taxes. And I, and many others, am stuck with assets that we now neither want nor can discard. I can't exactly relocate the court into a different jurisdiction. I hope that President Obama understands that, we don't all live in Wyoming; while upper income Federal taxes have been reduced, this is more than offset in many jurisdictions by the increase in non-deductible State, local and property taxes. And these taxes will only increase, as will the cost of protecting assets, in a socially challenged world. I have not totally dismissed the idea of tearing down my award winning home.

I have the pleasure of interacting frequently with Frank Sixt, Li Ka-shing's legendary financier. Li Ka-shing is not only the wealthiest man in Asia, he is also its largest property owner. Obviously, Frank has a vested interest in anticipating asset values. He worries that the risk/return relationship of assets does not internalize sustainability factors (climate change, water, biodiversity) relevant to both the creation and use of these assets. The majority of the world's CO2 comes, not from automobiles (9%), but from buildings (52%). But the mispricing is more than environmental. Technologies adapt so much faster than fixed assets (vacation homes were once mostly about establishing relationships in a second community; how frustrating is it to watch your children spend much of their vacation time maintaining global relationships on Facebook). And if fixed assets no longer provide generational satisfaction, then Frank worries whether there is a fundamental misallocation of assets.

I am not saying that we should live in an asset-less world. In a business context, there must ultimately be assets but they should be located where they are most appropriate. Putting aside the environmental damage, China can build fixed assets way more efficiently than anyone in the world (I recall my dear friend, Zhang Xin, who, twenty years ago worked in a Hong Kong factory sewing buttons on men's shirts and now is the largest upscale real estate developer in China, showing me the construction of her first apartment edifice. I marveled at the thousands of construction workers which she dismissed exclaiming, "Wait until you see how many are working at 2 am"). Not everything fixed is about China. Aluminum smelters and server farms should be placed at the cheapest source of energy, like geothermal in Iceland. We are a country that should only reluctantly possess fixed assets. Our challenge, for which I have no answer, is that humans accompany assets and, even independent of fixed assets, the internet and near zero cost of global telecommunications assures that the most efficient pocket of human talent will be accessed independent of where it is located. Phonetag may be a U.S. company, but I can assure you that the individual who transcribes my voicemail is not.

In a world of compressing asset values, in a world where retirement will no longer be government assured, in a world where technology makes it possible, it behooves us to wean ourselves from equating asset ownership with success.

85. Try not to confuse surviving with living. My hematologist is quite perturbed that I still ski. He worries that an irresponsible snowboarder will plow into me and cause fatal internal bleeding.

I have my own sense of the line that separates living from surviving; I have a clear objective of hugging that line.

I do, however, ski the earliest runs. The snowboarders aren't yet awake or, more likely, haven't even gone to bed yet.

86. Record your journey. I think my most sustained mistake is that, when young, I never documented my journey while it was occurring. I now remember my life in the context of facts and not, as I wish I did, its subtleties and ironies.

My diary is more than an attempt to record my daily routine. Forget posterity. It is a way I come to terms with life's wildcards. Recently, I was questioned by eight overzealous police as I walked across the George Washington Bridge on my way to a doctor's appointment. Apparently my walk was a bit meandering and the police viewed it with suspicion. I tried to be aware of the exact circumstances, not in order to report anyone, but because I knew that this episode would make a terrific entry in my diary; it is, however, difficult to absorb all the subtleties when your hands are handcuffed behind your back and your face is pressed against the fence.

I plead with my children to take a little time each day to record their lives. But they profess to be too busy living it to record it. I suspect that they will make the same mistake as did I.

87. But don't forget that records, particularly in a digital world, are permanent. George Kern, whom I met while advising (in a junior capacity) Grand Metropolitan in its hostile bid for Liggett & Myers, was the lead corporate lawyer for Sullivan & Cromwell. Sullivan & Cromwell is a highly prestigious law firm whose clients start, and often end, with Goldman Sachs. Grand Met was the leading purveyor of (alcoholic) beverages. It wanted to recover its rights to the US market, which were then owned by Liggett. Morgan was an equal opportunity hired gun. We did hostile transactions to and from the US and London.

Yet George, like most everyone on these precedent setting UK transactions, was a character. For starters, George was a pioneer in sartorial indifference.

Board meetings started early and at one such meeting, the seminal one, it was clear that George had not slept the prior night. In fact, it was clear that he had not been to his room. He had been out all night gaming (British for gambling). His outerclothes were rumpled and stained and were clearly not changed from the day before. Nor, I suspect, were his inner clothes.

He was the lead counsel for Grand Met so at one point, naturally, was asked to opine to the Board one last time on what they could expect once they launched a hostile bid.

George was brilliant and bombastic. We were all "miked" except George. In the middle of an insightful, if not slightly disoriented presentation, George looked down to notice that his tie was covered with his spittle.

Not missing a beat, he dunked his entire tie in the pitcher of water, which was in front of all our seats, and, as he lectured, patted his tie with his unused napkin.

I tell you this story not just because George was my fashion role model. It was also George who explained to me in the late 1970's the importance of envisioning every note that you ever write beginning with the phrase "Your Honor". I learned of the permanence of writing long before there was email.

If you ever visit my office, which I doubt either us ever will, you will notice that it is the extreme of minimalism.

I have an oversized desk which, while now suffocating my office, once fit comfortably into my then larger room. It serves as a visual reminder of how far down my career has sunk. I have a collage that I created where the tiles are pictures of all the scandals of the last decade; working together, they meld into an image of Madoff. I have a lucite cube from Tom Petters. Tom is the Farrah Fawcett of the business world; his mistakes, while significant, were overshadowed immediately – Farrah Fawcett's death by that of Michael Jackson and Tom's duplicity by that of Madoff.

But I keep no deal papers; that's someone else's responsibility.

TWELVE

THE UNITED STATES

And while proselytizing, of course I have views on the prospects for our country.

88. Our political system is inherently dysfunctional as the time frames of the challenges exceed the time frames of elected office. The real issues confronting our country (underfunded state pension liabilities, Medicare, the environment...) have time frames that exceed that of elected officials (2, 4, or 6 years). It is impossible that they will make rational decisions. The bailout had tacked on numerous items of self agenda; it was incredibly disappointing to watch our leaders fail to pull together in time of real crisis. Of course it's equally discouraging when our citizens buy gas inefficient cars once the cost of gas has receded. I wonder what Lee Kuan Yew is doing?

89. To postpone addressing our most fundamental problems is to allow the disintegration to accelerate. Regrettably the challenges noted above disintegrate at an accelerated pace when not addressed. In some cases, like the environment, they may reach a point of no return.

90. Our racism, while not overt, is structural. Gary Parr and Bill Lewis are two of the finest human beings, and bankers, that you will ever want to meet. In February 1997, Bill, who is black, and Gary, who is white, were asked to co-head Morgan Stanley's global merger and acquisition department. Bill called Gary that afternoon and asked, seeing as they didn't then know each other well, would Gary "please be gentle with this country boy from Richmond, Virginia". Gary explained that, while this approach might work with anyone else from Morgan Stanley, it wouldn't really work with him – Gary was not only from Virginia, but from the same town. In fact, it turns out that, with a year separation, they were born in the same hospital – except that Bill was born in the "colored wing".

Thankfully, these days are long gone (if you want more irony, Bill was identified by A Better Chance and was educated at Andover; at the same time, Gary was educated at the public school that became the fault line for desegregation).

Like many, I have asked what role there is for various organizations that protect the rights of African Americans when we now have an African American President. It has been explained to me that, while overt racism is largely past tense, structural racism is not.

The US is unique in that its local property taxes fund education. To the extent that education is the only equalizer (remember the first scenario), this is inherently a negative feedback loop. And add to that the inflexibilities of the teachers' union and you begin to realize just how challenging this educational issue will be.

91. The US currency is disdained - but the assets underneath our currency are not. It's hard not to be pessimistic on the US dollar. Our spending is reckless and it has been supported largely by one country, China, which has long but finite patience. I knew that we were in serious trouble when I met my friend's grandmother in Kazakhstan. She had stopped hoarding dollars under her mattress and was now hoarding Euros.

Sam Zell best explained to me our mutual relationship. China is the dentist and we are the patient. When he's about to drill, we grab the dentist by the genitals and say, "We're not going to hurt each other now, are we?"

But as much as foreigners don't want to hold our currency, they love our natural and human assets. They seek our citizenship which, more than anything, is a consequence of our reverence for upward mobility (again, remember how this story begins). Yet, for most of this decade, we humiliated foreigners at our borders and forgot that a country's reputation is developed when you enter and leave. We prevent them from converting their cash to our assets at great peril.

92. The clarity of the US legal system is underappreciated until you try doing business in the rest of the world. I own assets around the world. It is rarely a source of outsized returns and always a source of grief. It's not the language – it's the legal system. We can complain about our litigious society but there is amazing value in having a well established legal system.

93. A number of our most pressing challenges have relatively simple fixes, if we have the political willpower to pursue them. Upgrade the age of Medicare and Medicaid. Shut the postal system and give an internet connected computer to those that don't have one. Allow immigrants citizenship if they buy a house. Convert automobile engines such that they will run on our abundant supply of natural gas. Such simple ideas. They will never happen. The disadvantaged few will bullet vote.

94. The US is uniquely resilient. Technology is the answer to all our problems and, in this endeavor, the US remains uniquely positioned. We will never be surpassed in technology – our educational institutions, our culture, our lifestyle, our embrace of work ethic and upward mobility assure that.

Unprecedented in this world, we have an asymmetrical regard for success and failure- we respect success but, so long as there is effort, don't disrespect failure. This mentality is entirely disconnected from the rest of the world. Despite his incredible achievements, the parents of our boarder cannot acknowledge publicly that their son is out of a job. Having long dated an Asian woman, I have heard frequently about the importance of preserving "face". These are the cultural mindsets that discourage risk taking around the world; for us it engenders an entrepreneurial environment in which technology is the punch line to all our challenges.

With all our technological advantages, the only issue is, whether technology will provide answers before the problems become unsolvable.

THIRTEEN

SPIRITUALITY AND FINALITY

And finally, with a little time before the sun sets, I would like to offer some views on spirituality and finality.

95. The greatest gift is to confront perishability and then live decades thereafter. I truly believe that I awake differently than others. Having nearly lost life on a number of occasions, I believe that I awake with a wonderment and appreciation that others don't have. I have the luxury of not getting bogged down by life's annoying details, and I don't. I believe that I've been given the greatest gift - a visceral sense of perishability. How much better is this than those who come to this insight only when it's too late (such as going down in an airplane)? Regretfully, this mentality can't be taught – either you've experienced it or you haven't.

96. Probability determines much of our station in life.
I try to remember that what differentiates me from others is the circumstances into which we were born. That the maid cleaning my carpet could, under different birth, have been me and vice versa. I may have worked hard but so too has she. And she has undoubtedly sacrificed more for her family than I ever will for mine. With this mentality, there is no room for arrogance.

97. I previously misspoke – the gift of one's organs is the other lasting legacy. It's a pretty finite vision of G-d to believe that, in the next "life", you will need your organs. Upon adulthood, make organ donation an "opt out", not "opt in" decision.

Of course, the greatest gift is donating an unnecessary organ when still alive. When we were still clinging to medical optimism, I watched when my brother Steve's friend, Larry, offered to give Steve one of Larry's functioning kidneys. My role, unable to donate myself, was to modulate Steve's enthusiasm on the belief that, in the end, it would never happen. But, like a daredevil bungee jumper off a New Zealand bridge, Larry never hesitated nor wavered. Larry, a very talented lawyer in a shrinking industry, now spends his days looking for a job, which leads into my next point.

98. Don't anticipate G-d's intervention; we've already been given a most extraordinary gift. I live my life with the premise that G-d has given us one and only one gift – probability. That this amazing construct, with feedback loops but without interference, dictates all events in our lives. This is not the statement of a non-believer; it is the statement of a believer in awe of a uniquely powerful gift.

99. An unplanned finality negates an otherwise happy life. I have had the sadness of delivering two eulogies in the last three months. The first was for my twin brother and the second was for my only aunt. They died very different deaths.

I had closure with both. Over years of intimacy, we left nothing unsaid. I wish that I could say the same for my mother who, while still with us physically, because of advancing Alzheimer's, is no longer with us cognitively. My Dad, too, had closure with Steve and he now devotes all his time to the well being of the woman for whom he once would not buy a lift ticket. My first observation is easy – leave nothing unspoken.

But they died very different deaths. Steve died, at his own volition, quickly and with dignity. Since his late teens, his juvenile diabetes was such that he had lost one organ after another. He was the equivalent of a slab of cheese at a crowded cocktail party. He had carved a satisfying life but enough was enough. He said all his goodbyes and then, under hospice care, stopped his dialysis. Within two days he was gone.

My aunt, in contrast, never had the courage or foresight to deal with end of life issues. She never left a DNR (do not resuscitate) or a living will. The doctors were legally compelled to keep her alive for over a year of advanced bone marrow cancer as she alternated between whimpering and moaning; in one year she gave back an entire life of happiness.

With this experience, it was so discouraging to watch the Republicans accuse the Democrats of "killing grandma" and the Democrats running away from it. The financial implications of keeping an aged person, one who has lived well beyond their expected life, alive for an extra month are enormous; it's appropriate that the next generation knows what it cost them to help grandma pursue her futile wish for immortality.

But forget about the financial—out of compassion, it is cruel to keep people alive unnaturally. I hope that I remember this when it is my turn.

≈

That's the distillation of my 50 years of insights. I've had more than thirty years of a front row seat to the redefinition of both Wall Street and the venture industry, sometimes as an observer and sometimes as a participant. And, much of the time, I've had to wrestle with my own personal challenges.

Despite the fact that I'm donating all the proceeds from this book to charity, I doubt I'll sell many copies. My writing, amortized over 50 years, will not, in the end, turn out to be a very generous endeavor. That's ok – these observations, as I said, were compiled for my children.

The sun has now set. With pride I approached but never reached 100 observations. Remember what I said about my disdain of arbitrary numbers; if nothing else, I'm not a hypocrite.

Epilogue

Self publishing combined with digital technology makes for a dynamic process. To my assistants' annoyances, you need never finish writing your book. The feedback I get, whether praise or condemnation, is apt to be a couple of versions out of date.

And it is with this confluence of technologies that I can end the book with a variation of how it started - "What have I learned by writing this book?"

-That I'm way less secure than I thought. I still spend way too much time wondering whether those who don't critique my book do so because they didn't read it or didn't like it.

-That most everyone has deferred recording their own journey and most everyone now endeavors not to do so.

-That, while I would prefer this statement not be tested, I would choose to live an interesting life rather than a lucrative one.

The book has been read materially more than it has been purchased. The most effusive readers have conveyed their excitement by giving the book to their children. I'm flattered but please do buy them their own copy (search on lulu.com or go to "bit.ly/rlessin"). All the proceeds from the sale of this book go to George Jackson Academy (www.gjacademy.org). Everyone who was given this book is broadly connected, both physically and electronically. If so inclined, please leverage your connections.

George Jackson Academy is an institution dedicated to prosecuting my first observation – that intellectual over privilege combined with economic under privilege is a "killer" combination. This school educates the poorest and most intellectually gifted boys in New York City. It educates young men who, to its credit, the public school system disgorges as beyond their ability to teach. Yet George Jackson, like many wonderful charities, finds itself in very difficult financial condition. In an increasingly polarized "Glenn Beck" world, we need to support children who, from their youth, are trained to understand that there are two legitimate sides to every argument.

Publicly acknowledging the setbacks in my life has encouraged others, albeit privately, to reveal the setbacks in theirs. After reading the book, a classmate confessed to missing our 25th Harvard Business School reunion because his boss would not let him out of work. But this was not because he was in the middle of an intense transaction but rather because, having lost his job, he was unpacking parcels on the night shift for UPS. His Teamster contract didn't allow missed days for Business School reunions. Yet, even then, he and his wife opened their home each week to homeless children from the local shelter.

And it is selflessness like this that puts donating the proceeds from a book in its proper perspective.

Acknowledgements

With special thanks to Caitlin Yardeny who worked with me tirelessly to make this book a reality.

With great admiration for Andre Agassi who, while we never have met, showed me how one can leverage greatness into goodness.

And, most importantly, to my twin brother, Steve, who taught me the importance of perseverance and dignity. He will never read this book, which he largely inspired. I wish we could have discussed it; we both would have enjoyed that immensely.